NORTH

Poems by Cecelia Frey

*For Joan
Thanks for your
support.
Cecelia*

⬥ **BAYEUX ARTS**
DIGITAL-TRADITIONAL PUBLISHING

NORTH: Poems by Cecelia Frey

Copyright © Cecelia Frey, 2017

Publication: March 2017

Published in Canada by
Bayeux Arts Digital-Traditional Publishing
2403, 510 – 6th Avenue, SE
Calgary, Canada T2G 1L7

www.bayeux.com

Book design by Lumina Datamatics

All rights reserved.
No part of this book may be reproduced or transmitted in any form or by any means, electronic or mechanical, without permission in writing from the publisher.

Library and Archives Canada Cataloguing in Publication

Frey, Cecelia, author
   North / poems by Cecelia Frey.

ISBN 978-1-988440-02-6 (softcover)

   I. Title.

PS8561.R48N67 2017   C811'.54   C2017-900393-3

The ongoing publishing activities of Bayeux Digital-Traditional Publishing under its varied imprints are supported by the Canada Council for the Arts, the Government of Alberta, Alberta Multimedia Development Fund, and the Government of Canada through the Book Publishing Industry Development Program.

 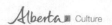

Printed in Canada

Acknowledgements

Thank you to the immigrants, including my grandparents, who built this country. It couldn't have been easy.

And, as always, thanks to the Calgary poets, a constant source of inspiration. Special mention must go to Vivian Hansen who read the manuscript and advised.

Barbara Allisen generously gave her permission for use of family history information. Thank you Barbara.

Dedication

For my grandmothers:
Tamar Woolsey O'Shea and Louise Montgomery McClintock

NORTH

NORTH

It's complex in its simplicity.

(Renate Kaiser, *Gaspesie Poems: Christopher Frey*)

inside a house a woman raises her head

> I come from huge silences.
> (Robert Kroetsch, *Letters from Salonika*)

    the space around her
                      still
                              still
            still
stillness as presence
                      silence
        as body
matter/molecules
        molecules
                thick   so thick
you could cut with a knife

you can hold in your hand
        taste
            touch
                  smell
the silence we are born into

the dogs behind the stove stiffen their ears

    something is out there
    something is coming
    something is about to arrive

any moment all hell's gonna break loose
once it was a cyclone
    ripping through
        carrying off the chicken coop
            chickens inside
once it was wolves
    gaunt haunched
  yellow eyed   relentless gait
      fur bristles scraping frigid air
  marking silence with rhythmic panting
        hungry for anything they could find

so much
    undefended territory
        hundreds of miles in any direction
            stillness spilling over the brim of any horizon

as her granny often said

    you never know what's galloping toward you in this life

but who is this woman

    we haven't heard from in years

        why does she stand in the middle of an empty room

where the children used to play

    what has she been doing

        since the ballerina pirouetted

            since the music box closed

since the children who knelt to float boats in spring runoff

                      left

has she been hiding in a coma

    or frozen in a snow drift

metabolism so low the organism needs neither nourishment nor drink

thawed out apart from malnutrition in pretty good shape except

for a few minor problems like chronic confusion and depleted brain function

inside a house a woman raises her head

horses pound into the clearing

                    snorting and pawing the winter ground*

* Jan. 15, 1920. The men have been gone with wagon & horses since day before yesterday to get a load of tamarack logs for the barn. 40 below on the outside thermometer and our nearest neighbour 10 miles, me without horse or wagon. Alone with the kiddies, evenings I knit and sew . . . I was relieved to hear the bells on the horses and then the men's voices calling directions unloading the wagon. I made them supper before Bill & Hugh pulled out for home. I hoped they would stay long enough to play the new song Celia sent from Spokane but they wanted to get home before night came on with more bitter cold.

1

O
Od(e)
Odysseus
ever returning

(George Woodcock, *Odysseus Ever Returning*:
Essays on Canadian Writers and Writing)

sun through autumn leaves

apple and elm and sun
              low on horizon
the image
      opens
            into
a city
a northern city
a northern city in summer

what sprouts in the dark
      rich black loam called them from across the sea
across continents, those thousands of immigrants looking for land
tulip bulbs dormant through a mean Arctic winter
beneath three feet of snow, lashings of wind, plan their strategy
sleeping and yet not sleeping, dreaming backward toward identity
forward toward direction, inner energy calling 'come'
come strength to awaken
            come force for the great push
                    up   up   up
                          break earth's thick membrane

start with the garden, equilibrium's green tree
    sweet peas along a wire fence
    gooseberries back of the shed
        green and purple-veined fish eyes
    down the path through a tangle of pea vines
        carrot tops trellised beans parsley shawl
    sleep in poplar's dappled shade
evening's long northern light:
    a small woman pulls weeds:
        bent from the hip, stick legs child drawn
        one arm on thigh, one arm reaching down
            earth   root   soil

this woman who came here to be my grandmother. all i saw:
    droopy stockings and beaded slippers and
        saggy sad lined face, loose-jowled chewing her supper

summer in the city:
    you could fry an egg on the pavement
    creosote of telephone poles mixing with cotton candy
    walking down 94th to the movies on 18th avenue
        saturday's serial, tarzan, hopalong cassidy
        men in rolled-up shirt sleeves selling tickets
            tobacco, licorice pipes, bags of jellybeans

      you could finger like prayer beads in the dark
         waiting for the movie to start
we leave the old man sitting in his horsehair easy chair
  strewn around with newspapers...

grandfather, dapper in his youth:
  curled moustache, fine dark eyes, jaunty straw
    tapping his heels down the sunny sidewalk
    swinging his sample case:
      hairnets, berets, bobby pins, safety pins, buttons
    under a relentless blazing prairie summer sun
      saplings on the boulevard
        moist and green smelling of new wood
    a horse drawn buggy on the avenue, clip clop of shod feet
they build a house around a piano:
  hammers drumming improvise
  brothers working side by side
    get together lumber and nails and up she goes
    raise high the roof beams carpenters
  innocent happy unmarked faces pose on second-storey framing
    confident they will shape the world to their vision
      as they shape this house to their plan
    standing before a stud and beam cross
       one squints against the sun

1914 population 72,516; 1916 - 54,000; 1918 - 53,000. real estate boom ends suddenly. city's population declines sharply. population and economy doesn't recover until WW2.

1915 North Saskatchewan River floods 14 metres. One infant drowns, and nearly 800 families lose their homes.

1920 Edmonton Symphony Orchestra holds first performance.

1920 Edmonton municipal election held December 13 to elect a mayor and six aldermen to sit on Edmonton City Council... voter turnout 54.6%... in the election's only plebiscite, Edmontonians rejected a proposal to pay their aldermen.

1923 Edmonton Grads win World Basketball championship.

December 13, 1926. Plebiscite whether the mayor should hold office for 2 years rejected.

February 27, 1927. Frank Hicklin, male, age 33, hanged at Provincial Gaol, Fort Saskatchewan for murder of wife July 12, 1926, throat cut.

1929. First licensed air field in Canada, Blatchford Field, commenced operation. "Wop" May and Max Ward use Blatchford Field as major base for distribution of mail, food, and medicine North.

1931 Edmonton municipal election held Wednesday November 11. Electors on list 42,753; votes cast 22,583; turnout 52.8%; cost $5,773.86; plebiscite held on whether aldermen should receive payment for their services rejected.

April 7, 1936. Student strapped for imitating Popeye.

1937 Edmonton's hottest temperature is recorded as 37.2 degrees on June 29.

the boulevard trees grown large, in their shade:
    an old man with cane shuffles along the sidewalk
        turns in at the gate of 11408. stops on the verandah
            removes his hat, mops his brow
    the man with small tight mouth is startled by the children
        with sweet pea lips popping up from bushes

sneaking upstairs on a hot summer afternoon:
    in a close and stuffy corner
    sun's rays funnelling dust motes toward it like a ray gun
    grandfather's retired sample case
    leftovers from his door-to-door salesman days:
        lifting the cover of the magic barrel
                slowly

        the moment before discovery the breath-holding moment
        reaching in my hand and out comes...
                Princess Patricia hairnets stretched on cardboard head shapes
barettes of various and wonderful designs and colours clipped ten to a card
                trinkets and oddities mysterious
                taking me to a place where
you don't have to eat bread soaked in oatmeal porridge before going to
church on Sunday where you look up all the hymn numbers on the board
behind the minister's head before the service even starts and spend the
remaining hour measuring footsteps of a fly on the pew in front of you
which makes you think of your aunt's kitchen on the farm. a fly on a half-
eaten bun whisks its forelegs together. the smells of slop pail, churn,
separator clear as clear on a Sunday morning in a church in the city.

there in the upstairs bedroom where i get into things
        (what else is there to do on a hot afternoon during the summer holidays)
            i drape myself in beads and bangles and fan dangles
                strut like the queen of Sheba in saturday's matinee

across a narrow hall:
        two beds. one for grandpa, one for granny and me
covers pulled up over our faces to keep out the night air even in summer
sound of bedsprings creaking in the night with the shift of bodies, of coughs
        sighs and grandpa's breathing sounding like the bubbling gas jet

                    until granny shouts over at him to turn on his side
the smell of stale bed covers, of scarf of bodies and hair and hairbrushes on the
dresser, of peppermints and gingersnaps beneath a wrinkled pillow slip and
in the warm and close dark a hole into another world opens at the bottom
      of my brain and like Alice i slip through. and sleep.

winter is flowerpots along the window sill:
      rusted tin cans set on chipped saucers
            scraggly deformed geraniums
                  african violets limp and longing for light
evenings is dominoes
      on the cloth under the paper shaded light bulb:
           the old woman with still-black hair
                streaked with grey parted in the middle draped
                    back to ubiquitous bun specs hooked
                      on beak. like a squirrel squirrels acorns
                        hides dominoes in her apron.

there once was an old woman
            i did not see
now i bend at the hip to root weeds from my garden
      pull the bedclothes over my head even in summer
           winters hide dominoes in my apron

2

> Ballyconnell 30th May 1913
> Mr. A.H. McClintock, Bank of Commerce
> Swan River. Manitoba Canada
> My dear Lex. I hope your well. Auntie and I
> were at Taylors yest. eveng. I cycled Smiths this
> morng with a wire. Louis.

they are standing at an open gate
as if they could step through or turn back
toward the house, two-foot-thick stone walls
vines that start from old growth each season.
the grass is cut, the hedges trimmed
a butterfly net leans against the wall near an open door.
back of the house is a mill and stream powering a millstone
grinding grain for this family for a hundred years

      behind them the table is set for tea
embroidered cloth, china cups and saucers
set as the scene is set
such certainty of serenity.
perhaps it is Sunday
perhaps they have just come from church in the village a mile distant
they seem to be wearing their Sunday best

aunt nellie in long dark skirt, white starched shirt
                         high collar, brooch at the throat
great grandmother frail and saintly draped all in black
great-grandfather with trimmed beard and watch chain.
standing apart, the hired girl in spotless white frock and apron

the man at the gate with jaunty moustache, fine features
suit, vest, shirt, tie, altogether snappy natty, is smiling
the woman is holding up a child
in white pinafore and sun hat.
what are they thinking
these two, this very moment
       might they be trying to decide
whether or not to follow their eldest son
who writes from his bank job in Manitoba
about great opportunities in Canada

i want to say to them don't do it.
stay where you are.
this country will chew you up and spit out your bones.
I want to go up to them
across the mowed grass, past the children's dog cart
in the tranquil Sunday afternoon
i want to shout into their blank foolish faces

their blind eyes looking past me
their stupid oblivious optimism
say: this country will do terrible things to you
you will have such sorrows you cannot imagine
you are going to see the child in your arms die

but I don't.
it wouldn't make any difference
they will do what they are going to do
the way the future is always calling
pulling us through a narrow wormhole
of inevitable days and years

3

>Ayr, 4 15 PM Jy 14/13
>Mr. A. McClintock, Bank of Commerce
>Swan River. Manitoba Canada
>Dear Lex. Here we are had a beautiful sail. Jack was sick, we are having a splendid day. After visiting Burns Cottage will send papers & acc of journey home. Hugh

    the call of the other room
             the one we step into

fact:
when we go from one room to another the mind engages itself with the immediate causing us to forget why we came
fact:
the highest immigration figures of our history
were just before the first world war

she did not see my sun until her 45th year
the brilliant foliage of my elm and poplar shifting colour in season
my prairie blizzard and forty below and going into the long dark tunnel of winter
my summer heat enough to scramble a person's brains
my choking dust, blistering asphalt, scalding tar

she could not have known what she was getting into when she read the
advertisement on the village post office bulletin board. opportunity. free
land. she must have pictured
a meadow, green hills, gentle rains.
> she could not have imagined the sheer meanness of some weather
> > or the violence of some land.

she never saw her family again
nor the view of Ballyconnell from Daisy Hill
nor the pork market in the square saturday mornings

she left behind graves of daughters
to answer the call of the unborn
she took the complexities of the crossing upon herself
> the weight of the future

take only what you cannot leave behind
> they told her at immigration

she stepped into a new land
carrying a piano on her shoulders

4

> 4/8/15 Mr. A.H. McClintock, Bank of Commerce,
> Winnipeg, Canada. Thank you so much for letter. I
> am forwarding you copies by mail. It's too bad I
> cannot send... Auntie Nelly. Ballyconnell

she lived with Dostoevsky and Tolstoi
saw Joyce die and be born a few miles from where she was a girl of
thirteen rolling hoops in wide circles
middle-aged when the Titanic went down
she saw the start and finish of both world wars
and all the other wars in between
Boer, Korea, just missed Viet Nam
passed from candlelight to electricity
from Sunday gossip after church to the telephone,
      from dog cart to airplane

i was too young to care or even consider that she had a life
somebody else told me how she took time off
from clerking in her husband's drapery establishment
to go upstairs and birth one of my uncles
and about when
she nursed the hired girl through erysipelas then carried death in her hands
to her own child crying in the next room

i never asked the questions
i had no intention of dragging the weight of history along with me
i stood before her wearing the highest red heels I could find
(how're y' gonna walk in those things?)
impatient for the boy waiting at the door
holding in his outstretched hand
        an air fern in a glass bubble

i left her cooling her tea in a saucer
        beaded slippers set on a cushion
        stockings like loose bandages
        falling on her child-drawn stick legs

2

I'm going way out west to where the buffalo used to roam,
I'm going to try to settle down, and build myself a home.
(folk song)

lost in trees

for tamar o'shea

first sighting of the savage country
                               trees
aspen poplar, scrub willow, pine
         swirl around her with a sun gone crazy
         a surreal kaleidoscope
                 thousands of acres
                           trees free for the working
closing her in. she never thought them poetry
she might have thought poems more lovely
if she had come across some. nights
staring into dark
lying between husband and children
     in a tent
         the first summer
the end of a hundred miles of bad road
     trail so narrow
both sides of the wagon scrape bush
     wheels bump over fallen trees
         rocks
           deep ruts
                     mud holes

the horses toss their manes, swish their tails
        quiver their flesh against mosquitoes
        and that fierce lean fly
                the indians call bull dog

    A lean-to of canvas unrolled on the side of
    the wagon was home until a house of round
    logs and mud-plastered cracks was built
            (Barbara Allisen, *The Whole Fam Damily*)

        …four days later they had only
        travelled as far as Sangudo as the road was so
        muddy they got stuck several times…
                (ibid.)

he calls it paradise
but even paradise is a prison if there's no way out
as a desperate eve discovered
    before letting herself be seduced
maybe she didn't even like apples

it's all right for him
he shows those trees who's boss
tames them into houses

      cut 'em down
          run 'em through
      saw blade screaming
      stack 'em as lumber
hitches up a team of horses
pulls the stumps like so many rotten teeth

> Dan returned to the sawmill for a few
> months to get some money to live on. When
> he returned in the spring they began
> clearing and breaking. Murilla planted and
> tended a huge garden.
>
>   (ibid.)

she puts up a chicken wire fence
                states her terms
the trees answer
      send out secret underground tentacles
she takes to keeping an axe by the kitchen door
daily makes the rounds
            hacks those roots to bits
imagines them writhing in agony
                and smiles

no way out but by heaven.

she stands in the clearing
                    looking up
a small pretty woman with a great deal of hair
        pinned on top of her head
one arm shades her eyes
searches for breathing space
        a passage of blue
somebody get me out of here
she cries to a great horned owl
who one day floats into a giant spruce

        sits there for the longest time staring
              with his stern yellow owl eyes
every time she looks out her window there he is
              huge clawed feet diminishing branch
right at home as if he owns the place
            and all that is in it
                as if he owns the trees
the whole great northern boreal forest

tracking the self. she takes to writing a diary

i.

Good Friday. boiled up a boiler of turnips for the pigs . . .   Saturday. D went to Roch got repairs for disk, groceries, etc. I scrubbed floors, coloured eggs . . . Easter Sunday. Kids had egg hunt in morn. McClures were here in aft. We played bridge . . . Weather lovely. I practically finished Mary's coat and skirt. D went with lumber to Hansen's and didn't get home. It rained heavy in the night. I was very worried as it was very dark. . . . D set hen on turkey eggs. Weather raw. Mail day. I was hoping for a song from C. so far away in Spokane but didn't come . . .

ii.

April 18. Dan started disking. 1921 year on the land begins. 20) D took disk into town, got it repaired and sharpened. Sold some barley. 21 & 22) disking. 23) snow. 25) more disking. 26) snow. 27) D went to town to get plow fixed. May 2) Hugh and Katie arrived with horses and plow at 2 o'clock. 3) Nels arrived with seeder & seed at 10:45. Bill & L. arrived with horses at 11:15. The crop is going in fast. 4) Mike arrived about 1 o'clock with more horses & seed. 5) Finished putting in crop about 3 o'clock. I put in *my* garden. 14) Three turkeys hatched. I shot a little tiny egg off S.E. corner post from gate post. 15) We brought the three turkeys into house. Little hope for rest of birds.

iii.

June. Queenie bred & disking. I dug plant bed. Snowed   . . .   did big washing ironing. D worked all day on pump. cows beat it in evening . . . still raining . . . Marg brought up tomatoes and cabbages in evening, caught me out in the rain feeding chickens, slopping pigs . . . I was supposed to go to ladies tea in town but couldn't find horses in time . . . Still raining. . . Marg. came in morn & went for mail on Babe. . . got red cabbages from Marg. . . I planted cucumbers after soaking since Sunday. also we planted peas in even. . . I sowed rest of marrows in front of house. They were well sprouted. . . I set out 64 cabbage plants that Marg. brought over. Traded seeds with Lily in even. . . plants *up* in my garden.

blood on snow

1

morning
        early winter
we're sitting around the kitchen table
Dan in his long johns and trousers
he was running a mill with the trees he cleared on his quarter section
Tom Nogorty was out early to get a load of lumber
when we saw out the window a white-tailed deer
come bounding over the rise in back of the house
well Dan sprung up grabbed his gun off the wall
was outside quicker'n you can say jack robinson
had the gun up and cocked and off in one motion
                              whack of rifle
                                  crack of air
and there y'were boys
        grub for the winter

i remember yor poppa standing there shivering
        pants around his ankles
                he got so excited seeing that deer
he forgot he didn't have his suspenders up

i remember, pipes up Mary
the old farm, the house back from the road
there's a picture around some place
momma and me and dad with his gun
standing behind the deer lying in the snow

I was ashamed to show that picture
to my friends at nursing school
my father in his long underwear
we made him put on a jacket for the picture

> They loaded their furniture and some
> carpenter's and woodsman's tools in a
> covered wagon and bought a plow.
> With four horses and a cow they
> started out for the Ronan district.
> Four days later they had only got
> as far as Sangudo as the road was so
> muddy they had gotten stuck several
> times. Here they got stuck again but
> could not wait for help as it might be
> a week before somebody came along.
> The lighter possessions were unloaded
> and the heavier furniture moved to

the back of the wagon. The horse managed to pull the front wheels out of the molasses-like gumbo but not the back ones so the furniture was shifted to the front. No sooner had the back ones been freed than the cow ran off. She was not found that day but the second one located her in a field with some other cattle. When Dan went to retrieve her the bull chased him out. A plan had to be devised as a cow was far too important to abandon. Alvin was elected to act as decoy. When he had lured the bull far enough away he climbed a tree enabling Dan to reclaim the cow. Two days later their road ended and a moose trail began. The wild life would have the best crossing of the Paddle River so even tho it was narrow and muddy it was quite shallow. The crossing had to be enlarged with axes and shovels to be wide enough for the wagon but the

      homestead was near enough to motivate
      the work.
      (Barbara Allisen, *The Whole Fam Damily*)

2

Mary's version

the first summer we lived in a tent
we had a cookstove that sat on the ground
      it looked strange
             a stove in the middle of nowhere
i still see my father sitting on a tree stump
      playing his mouth organ
we always had to have music
that was one thing we always had to have
      like the birds we had to sing
          against the silence

they came up from Washington
      dad with a lumber contract
well there was hardly a border in those days
      people crossed pretty much when they wanted to

Dad rented a railway car for twenty-five dollars
    travelled north to Edmonton on the Grand Trunk Railway

  we lived in Edmonton for a couple of years
the whole family worked at the tie camp
then war was declared and the contract cancelled
dad heard about homesteads north of here
    wagon piled high and four kids
i was the oldest of the new family. what i remember
    mile after mile watching the horses
        brown satiny rumps
            glistening in the sun

my grandfather came to the States during the potato blight of 1845-49
the British were after him so he had to leave
his wife
    that'd be my grandmother
        dared not go into the village
    for fear of getting beat up
        for letting her husband go to a heathen land
            a godless place of wild savages
after a while he was able to send for her and the children
my father that'd be Dan O'Shea
    was born in Chicago and grew up there

he moved west with his family to Minnesota where they took up farming
dad left home and went to Seattle
    where he got into the lumber business
       and met his first wife
           they had one child then divorced
dad and my mother met in Spokane
she had been married to a violinist who was a real rotter
       so the story goes

dad loved it here in the north
so what if you have to put up with forty below
      icicles hanging from the ceiling
        over your head where you sleep
we're free here he used to say
   free to freeze to death momma would answer
it was hard on her
dad had the challenge of beating down the land
   but this country made momma feel small
she had a fanciful nature
the Cree chief who came to visit and smoke with dad had it right
    imagination no good for the bush

   he appeared suddenly out of nowhere
      the first summer

                one hazy afternoon

                        a man on a horse

so silent

      as if silence was the natural state and all else silliness

he taught dad how to smoke the traditional pipe

they would sit cross-legged in the grass and pass it back and forth

           but as soon as the pipe business was finished

                he'd look at dad's home roll tin

once dad was in town and splurged on tailor mades

           well that chief thought he had died and gone to heaven

3

beeeeeee like I

hold your head up high

the wheel in the parlour goes round and round

        round and round

                round and round

where the door is kept closed

        on the cold linoleum

              that no one walks on

the stuffed chesterfield and chair

        that no one sits on

the piano that no one plays

the wind-up phonograph
        turns around in an empty room
the sharpener in the barn turns round
grandaddy's hands, joint-swollen
        sharpen skinning and gutting knives
                know the precise connecting point of blade and stone
grandaddy's large joint-swollen hands
        settle the delicate wood of violin
                between shoulder and chin
blunt callous-tipped fingers
        lower the bow exactly
                to quivering string

the maverick way

    it is 1920 and somewhere in Japan a woman is pouring tea. her hands are small and white and smooth. her fingernails are long and lacquered. she is kneeling on a mat. she is wearing a hand painted silk kimono embroidered with silver and gold threads. her black hair is sculpted high on her head and skewered with elaborate combs. her face is painted white, her lips brilliant red. the man for whom she is pouring tea sits opposite. he is very clean having just been bathed by the woman. he bows and takes the cup she offers in his two hands. she bows. he bows. he drinks. in one graceful flowing movement she lifts herself from the floor like a delicate bird rising and takes small steps on feet smaller than a child's. she is a finished work of art.

it is 1920 and somewhere in northern Alberta a woman is pouring tea. her hands are red and rough the nails jagged. she sits on a wooden chair before a wooden table roughly hewn from raw cut lumber taken from surrounding trees. she is wearing a loose dress made from flour sacks. her hair is gathered freely on top her head and stuck with hairpins. her cheeks are rosy. mornings she washes her face with snow. the man for whom she is pouring tea sits opposite. he smells of grain and wind and livestock. he is wearing stained coveralls, boots flecked with mud and manure. he hasn't had a bath in two weeks, the well has dried up and water has to be hauled from the river. the woman leans one hand on the table to lift her weight from the chair. her movements are heavy and awkward. any day now she will give birth to my mother. she stands solid on wide feet.*

*Aug. 6) took seeder to Millers. 7) Hoed potatoes. Went to river for wash water. 9) Alvin and I fixed fence at lake. 12) Dan worked on pig pasture fence. I milked both cows, separated and fed calves. 16) I did weeding in my garden and more sewing. 17) We moved calves to pig pasture. 19) It rained heavily. I cleaned house and scrubbed floors. Mary and I tried to put cows in meadow but cows ran all over farm. 23) Dan finished cutting and took binder to Charlie's. Alvin & I finished stooking in ev.

3

> Wherever you go
> there you are
> (original author unknown)

the family reunion

Is this it?
What's that?
There's no sign
Blew away in the wind
This can't be it
Bad winds last November. Blew an automobile clean off the road
This isn't what I remember
Did a flip-flop right inta d' ditch
This can't be right
Snapped Olaf Johnson's neck like it was a toothpick
Someone's supposed to meet me
Work of the devil, them automobiles. Revelations is at hand!

      (not much rail traffic these days
           people drive or take the Greyhound
but i want to recall those summers
    we came here as children:
mom packed us onto the train
           branch line going nowhere
                straw seats going backward
belted suitcases and bag lunch
           twelve-year-old Nellie in charge

conductor swaying along the aisle toward us
    that moment of fear
        when you were sure you had lost your ticket
settling into the clackety clack of the wheels
    prem sandwiches and nickel pop
        miles and miles and miles of nothing
            but boring barley and wheat and oats
                      and trees
        miles and miles and miles of trees)

one hallowe'en we tipped over his outhouse
    moaned and shrieked around his station
        where the CN let him sleep in a room at the back
he came out and fired his shotgun into the air
    and we ran screaming in all directions

today he looks through me toward the caboose
    disappearing into scrub and farm land
        (the amazing clearing of all those trees
            grandmother would have approved)

    maybe he's right   maybe i'm not here
        the way cells divide and are reborn
        maybe after fifty years i'm reconstructed

        a simulation, a ghost
           a gauzy filament floating
                between the here and now and the there and then

            certainly one of us does not exist
       the mind is not old home week
              but a mess of neurons and networks
      where physical presence has no place

maybe i never have been here
maybe i'm dreaming i'm here
i've been having strange dreams lately
dreams about losing things
              lecture notes, exam schedules
                  babies, poems
dreams about rooms, so many rooms make up a life

some dreams parts of me are blank, an arm
a leg, a gouge out of my torso, the left side
in the dream i search everywhere for my missing parts
        frantically
            without success

i came believing i would find myself sitting at the table

        instead i find a stranger in my place
i came believing i would find you
                alive and well and pouring sand through your fine hair

in the beer parlour

i ask about wine
        we got red and we got white says the waitress
                in tight jeans and shirt first three buttons undone
guess i'll have a beer i say

my cousin Harold says
        you should come home more often
        it's all changed now
        oil changed everything
there's the new Blue Sky motel on the edge of town
you couldn't get a room there even if you tried
all taken up with oil guys
and the Chinaman's is the Burger Baron
us old guys still meet there every morning about ten
                            to chew the fat
the young people go off to the university
                whether they need it or not

we raise our glasses to the way things used to be
                drink deeply

you remember Loretta Davis, Harold leans into it

        she was a Robertson, they farmed north of town
            you and Lottie were in the same grade
oh yeah i say wondering if she was the chubby blonde
            or the tall brunette
she went to the university Harold says
        became a nurse
           married Lester Davis
        they moved out to the Davis place near Dead Horse creek

well they got a divorce
        he'd turn on the TV and she'd switch it off
           and he'd turn it on and she'd switch it off
           and this went on all day
he told her to stop switching off the goddamn TV or he'd throw
    her outa the house
        so she drank a bottle of methanol she got at the hospital
           then she had second thoughts but he wouldn't drive her to town
    it was during the playoffs
        so she had to drive herself into emergency

well he always was lazier'n billy be darned
he took over the place from his folks
        but he didn't bother working it
it was well treed

    so he made a pretty good living cutting firewood

once i went out there to get a load
he was stretched out on the couch watching TV
    she was up fixing the roof

we stare into our beer
i'm still trying to figure out which one she was
    but blonde or brunette
        Loretta has passed into story.

aunt ida dishes the dirt

it's saturday afternoon and we're sitting around the beer parlour telling jokes at least the men are. randy's voice comes through the blue smoke haze telling the one about the guy who's had one too many and's driving home after the beer parlour closes and rolls his truck into the ditch and phones 911 on his cell. the operator naturally is trying to find out where he is. how many times do I have to tell you he shouts into his phone, I'm under the goddamned truck!

when ida comes in with her bags of groceries. this's kathryn's girl says my cousin harold oh yes I knew your mother well, she says, in the old days, I guess she's gone now, everyone's gone but me. my own mother too these ten years i can't believe it. three swings of the cat and a run around the table she'd say if we asked her what was for supper. so what do you do ida asks and i don't want to say poet. the word will hang heavy in the air above the table like an undigested lump of meat hangs heavy in the gut and besides it would only confuse ida for 'poet' is not a thing to be anywhere let alone in this place where even 'writer' seems pretentious. i write books i say figuring maybe she'll think cookbooks or such, but she comes back with isn't that lovely i always wanted to be a writer. Doris Burns is a writer, she wrote a book, have you read it, well it's the funniest thing, you remember Doris, her sister-in-law used to be Bernice Crowder who married Phil Burns her brother, he shot his wife and daughter, it was in all the papers, well, that was a few years ago, he always was crazy, well all of those Burns are, y'know, they have too much money for their own good but anyway this Bernice Crowder used to go out with a fellow named Peter Easter and we used to double date, I used to go out with this lawyer, this was a long time ago of course we used to have a whale of a time I'll say that but you see then she married Phil and then well he was really crazy brooding y'know from the start, they sent him to Rochester several times well of course they had the money but you know the two younger girls they were sleeping out in the yard or they woulda got it too...

i watch the pleats around ida's small prim mouth move her lips in and out like an accordion. i do the math. she was some years younger than my mother who would be ninety by now. she married a Robinson who lived on the next farm and the two women were great friends.*

yor poor mother, she had it tough, a single mom with three kids to raise and in those days no welfare. it was too bad about her getting sick and yor poor father too. well when the car went into the ditch they just about had to get married didn't they? in those days, not today of course, the young people sleeping all over the place with all sorts of people they don't know but things were different then. his mother that would be yor grandmother she took on something terrible about them spending the night together in the ditch, very proper she was, Presbyterian y'know, but they were planning on getting married anyway so i can't see what difference it made but you just wonder, if yor mother had married a man who had his health her life would have been different. . .

at the other end of the table the men's voices have increased in volume in proportion to the number of glasses in front of them. Steve is Ukrainian and likes to tell Ukrainian jokes on himself. did you hear the one about the Ukrainian kid who climbed up into a tree because he wanted to play with the Leafs? didja hear the one about. . .

*March 1. Ida came up and helped me wash. 2. I did all babys & kids washing & ironed. I scrubbed kitchen at night. The weather was colder. 3. The weather very cold. Louis came home from mill. 4. L. went to Roch. He paid what was left on Pollocks bill & some on our own. 5. I wasn't feeling well. Ida came in morn. and went for mail on Babe. I mailed an order for four song books. 8. L. went to Johnsons & got some carrots. I ironed & finished overalls for kids & rendered lard & mended. 11. Still not feeling well. Ida came up and stayed all aft. It was very cold.

(Diary of a farm wife. 1939)

mud

> March 30. Bob went for rest of lumber. I
> washed. 31. I finished washing. Louis & Bob
> went down with wagon & hauled lumber up but
> got stuck in field.
>
> (Diary of a farm wife, 1939)

then there was the wedding when we had to pick up flowers from Patsy's cousin's house and deliver them to the church we had to park half a block away because of the gumbo

and Reggie comes out the front door wearing army issue rubber boots his arms full of flowers and balancing himself on planks set down from porch to road stepping

carefully makes it partway before overbalancing and trying to right himself lurches too far the other way and does an outrageous slapstick dance while we in the car

hold our breaths and it was only by some miracle that he gets himself righted and continues along them boards slippery as pig grease and makes it to the car.

and was it that wedding or another, that bride or another, let the mud memories roll all together now down to the mire of impassable main streets. the time the bride in long white gown trailing veil clutching bouquet arrives at the church flung over her brother's shoulder like a sack of spuds and thank god as people said for months after

    he luckily and realistically was wearing his oil rig boots.

    and was it that wedding dance or another going home getting stuck in the mud par for the course as they say what with road conditions car conditions and flat tires it was

    only due to the good lord being willing and the creek not rising you got anywhere at all like the time of the sleet storm and the windshield wipers not working and Harry

    having to stick his head out the window to see where he was driving. no, no, someone says, we're telling mud stories here like the time Joe's car gets stuck coming home

    from the dance and we try to push it backwards and forwards digging it in deeper until it's up to the axle and joe says to hell with it, he'll have to come back with the horses

    in the morning so we take off our dancing shoes and nylons and slog through mud up to our knees our feet making sucking noises like in quicksand. dog tired we're some happy

    when by the light of the moon we see the farmhouse in the distance and someone says i can hardly wait to climb between the sheets. not my sheets, says Mabel, not with those feet.

since no one is about to start up the stove and heat water that time of night we wash at the pump water so cold it sends shock waves through us reverberating still down these many years.

oh I remember sister says. that was the time Lily always the one for dancing starts up. around and around the pump she goes and then the rest of us start too. dancing and singing and
carrying on under the moon like a buncha gypsies as mother would say in the morning.

i haven't been up here for a long time

but I remember the last time

wading through dust tumbleweeds
rolling out from under your bed
corners undisturbed for years
everything just as it was
when your folks sold up and moved to town
the new owners wanting only the land
your mom with just her suitcase
walked out one door and in another
her new house in town
where everything was spanking brand new and clean

even the heat of summer is the same
sun beating down on slanting uninsulated roof
and dead flies
        hundreds of carcasses on the windowsill
                on the floor beneath the window
a veritable fly graveyard

standing at your bedroom window looking out
    push rewind
        stop at homesick city kid

spooked by black and too much quiet
yearning for city lights
    midnight sirens
      street cars one block over
        rattling the window
          flung wide to catch an evening breeze

stop at apple orchard with swing
each summer the grass longer the trees less tended
more bruised apples forgotten on the ground
    swing/pendulum/clock run down
      slower and slower until one year stopped

and wild strawberries the taste on the tongue
    squeezing shut our eyes in pubescent ecstasy
      declaring the taste
        like drinking champagne
as if either one of us knew what that was like

and board walks in town
Wong's where everyone went after the Saturday night dance
    where no one asked me to dance because I was a stranger and also
      a fat twelve year old
        except one boy who you told to ask me

stuffed animals placed precisely on the bed
chenille spread pulled up and tucked beneath the pillows
      the way they taught us in home ec
painted bureau, embroidered runner, tin of face powder
          a tube of stale lipstick

was it by accident or design you did not return?
some people like to tell stories of where they're from
          what they've left behind
others step through a doorway
and the room they walk into is their reality

photographs stuck along the bureau mirror
      school girls laughing into the camera
          a ticket for the high school graduation dance

going to see the royal train at Evansburg, June 2, 1939

pussycat, pussycat, where have you been?

hooray it's a holiday
we're off to see the royal train
although nellie and i don't know what that is
but it has something to do with the king and queen
and the picture from the flour sack
framed and hung on the faded wallpaper
above the Winnipeg couch

> June 1. Lady had puppies. I run a nail in my foot. We got ready to go to Evansburg. June 2. We went to see Royal Train at Evansburg. Approx. five hundred people there. 3. Mike came back from coast. L. took post mall back to Scott's. All very tired. We heard Lily's birthday on radio. 4. Rain. Louis harrowed garden in morn. 8. Louis got sack of flour with picture of K & Qu. Also can of tobac for Bob.
> (Diary of a farm wife, 1939)

daddy puts on his suit and tie and momma
her dress with flowers and a flouncy
                          thing around the middle
baby is wearing her good bonnet
nellie and i our church dresses
which we don't get to wear very often
since we seldom go to church because
of weather or horses getting out
and chores and seeding and harvest
                              but luckily
we don't have to go
because we're protestants

momma packs a lunch of cold roast chicken
dad snaps the reins over the back of our team
and away we go although it's always uncertain
    how long it will take
        or if we'll get there
    so many things can go wrong
but that day things go pretty good
our white Babe prancing along right smartly
her brown sleek-hided colt running beside
the same colt that dies later in the summer
(Babe coming to the house one morning in an awful state

calling out my father to bring her colt back to life
to make him stand up and walk and whinny
but that is in both our future and Babe's future
the same way we have to leave the farm at the end of summer
because our father gets sick and dies
the same way in three month's time a war will be declared
and neighbours and neighbours' sons will be called out
and nothing will ever be the same
but the day we go to see the king and queen
we don't know any of this
so everyone including Babe is happy)

> April 17. We heard on radio
> that Hitler & Musolini had
> hesitated in making reply to
> Roosevelt in his request for
> a ten year truce. European
> situation looking bad.
> (ibid, 1939)

they come from as far as Grande Prairie to the north
Cache Creek to the south
buggies, wagons, a few jalopies
park in the long grass beside the tracks

kids swing down skinny brown legs
give each other the wary eye
        start chasing each other through the trees yelling like banshees
horses put to graze switch their tails
bees drone, crows caw, flies scream
        mosquitoes whine

then out come the picnic boxes
        cloths spread on the long grass
and the box cameras
and straightening up and standing still
when all you want to do is squirm and scratch
        and fall down and roll on the grass and shout and squeal
            we are
five hundred loyal subjects in royal spirits
        visiting, joking, laughing
        trading accents and crop gossip

the hour passes
someone hears on the radio that the train will be late
hot and itchy in the rail allowance ditch
in the prickly dry grass and scuttle of mice
another hour passes and another

Billy Mueller is the first to raise the alarm
smoke at the horizon
brags about it 'til his dying day
the crowd suddenly silent as holding air before a hailstorm

and on it comes
                    tons of relentless steel
a great huge oiled machine
black smoke and signature whistle call
singing of rails as it closes in. coming
                    coming
    swoosh
                          gone
five hundred held breaths let out
flags wave
    voices cheer
mothers hold up infants-in-arms
so they can see history in the making
so they can tell their grandchildren
they saw the king and queen

4

There's men that somehow grip your eyes,
and hold them hard like a spell
(Robert Service, *The Shooting of Dan McGrew*)

an edmonton story circa 1930

Frankie and Ollie were lovers
lordy how they could love
they met between rooms
>   in the hall of the rooming house
then he knocked on her door to borrow a cup of sugar
then she invited him in for a beer
he was quite the sharpie in spite of losing one arm in the hopper
>   working the threshing crew
>>   up around lac ste anne
he kept the empty sleeve so neatly pinned up
stepped so smartly down the avenue
in checkered jacket, straw, bow tie
spinning the shoeshine boy an extra dime

he took her to the movies, after
undressed her with his one good hand
>   with which he was amazingly adroit
then she found out he didn't have much money
except for what the company paid him for his arm
she wanted to do better than that since
all she had was the burnt-out relief

he told her she'd be sorry and she was
for then came the winter of thirty-three
a hard winter on the coldest corner of the world
ninety below with wind chill factor
she wasn't getting any younger
and her poor old nipples froze
when they failed to thaw out in spring
there was growing concern
one lover simply walked out, another
a stray who more or less wandered in
without understanding the situation
suffered from frostbitten lips

she was so lonely for Frankie
she looked for him everywhere
but she could weep and wail til the cows come home
that man took his one good arm to where it would be appreciated
a woman half his age with three kids to feed

now Ollie sits before her mirror
lifts her hair going thin and sighs
i'm not myself tonight

re membering Slave Lake

1

the laughing man

at the edge of grey blanket
between cool swallows of beer
on a hot August afternoon in 1946
in room 201 at the old Strathcona
he slaps his knee
to the rhythm of his song
    I'm in the jailhouse now
        I'm in the jailhouse now

i am ten years old and in love
    he is so handsome
wide cheek bones, black hair, straight nose
i don't know he's an indian
    the word has not entered my vocabulary
oh i know about indians
    having been born and bred in the territories
        but i don't know they are different than me
        (or i from them) until i move to the city
and go to the movies and find out that indians

    are the bad guys and come swooping over the hills
        riding bareback and naked and waving tomahawks
            whooping and hollering enough to scare the bejeesus out of you
still i don't connect those indians with Ray
on this hot August afternoon in 1946
in room 201 at the old Scona
Ray conducts the air with his bottle of beer
sways toward his Jenny
    if you were the only girl in the world

this hot August afternoon Ray is happy
    and maybe also a little bit drunk
        because he's celebrating being let out
            of the war which they let him fight
                even though he is an indian
but the real reason today
    Ray wouldn't call the king his uncle
        today he married Jenny
            a gentle woman with very white skin
                who he met in a boarding house last winter

this afternoon Ray has no plans
            but it so happens
    Ray is highly educated for an indian

so they let him have the job of indian agent
and Ray and Jenny move to Slave Lake

then the summer i am twelve and moping around the house
and eating chocolate bars and getting fat because my father has just died
and my older sister has just got a boyfriend
mom sends me to stay with Ray and Jenny
where my best friend is a girl from the village
who has a dad and a roly-poly baby brother and horses
and rides as though she's a growth on the horse's back
while i plop plop plop along beside her
riding our horses down to the lake
plunging our horses into the water
drying ourselves in the sun
Alice tells me stories about indians
how once they were warriors
kings of their own country
how the Cree liked to steal horses from the Blackfoot
late in the night they camped in the wooded hills
how they loved racing their horses
singing a horse song haw haw haw haw
escaping with horses and a blackfoot girl

that night i hear horses around the cabin

        galloping like thunder blown in and out with the wind
            first in the distance then closer closer
                then sounding like they're on top of me
                    then fading again into the dark
horses galloping in and out of my mind
   ridden by ghosts of warriors seeking revenge
      racing their horses late in the night
            riding low on their horses to make less of a target riding
      riding a short-tailed fine black horse red blanket flying

but no says Ray
      at breakfast next morning
          the horses are real
              indian ponies gone wild
                  they like to race in the moonlight
                      have one helluva time

Ray's face across the table
      innocently eating his cornflakes
                    dissolves
      eyes tranquil as a wood pond
                fire up
      nostrils flare
short military style haircut becomes

      long warrior braids hanging either side his head
                  Hollywood style

Ray is a bare chested bareback rider crouched low
      in full war paint and flying robes
          escaping with horses and a Blackfoot girl

2

Alice

After about the second week at Ray and Jenny's when i'm pretty much in the same rut i'd been in at home Jenny says 'we're going visiting this afternoon so maybe you'd like to get cleaned up & comb your hair.' We pile into the half ton cab, me in the middle which i hate
   because of having to straddle the floor gear shift which is embarrassing when you're twelve years old with an inflated sense of dignity. We drive to the village where the main street is
   a dirt trail & most of the houses are shacks or rusted out trailers with broken windows. But Ray stops the truck in front of what looks like a real house with a front yard of quack
   littered with dog bones & a fence of slats here & there hanging at odd angles. We follow the bones up the walk & onto the porch where a man with a paunch & a bottle of beer in his hand

says hello through the smoke of a cigarette hanging from his
bottom lip & the torn screen of a screen door. Inside there's not much
furniture & no curtains & fat little kids with shy smiles
    like their dad's & yipping dogs rolling & tumbling all over the place.
The mother in jeans & t-shirt & bare feet calls into a back room & a girl my
age comes through the door &
    that's the first time i lay eyes on Alice

> Alice laughing with saskatoon juice on her chin.
> brown-eyed sun-dappled brown face through
> trembling aspen. jam cans strung across our
> saddles. searching out the best bushes with the
> plumpest juiciest fruit.

who coached by her mother says 'do you want to see the horses' so i say
'yeah, sure' so we go
    out back. She walks lightly & sways gracefully which makes me
feel even flabbier plumper & pasty white. So there we are standing around
in the corral talking to the horses &
    occasionally to each other when she says 'wanta go for a ride.' i
had been on top of a horse exactly once before in my life at one of those
places where you pay a quarter to ride some
    poor nag around in a circle about three times which if nothing
else made me realize it's a long way from the top of a horse to the ground.

But i'm thinking Alice will find it very amusing

    if i'm scared of a horse so i say 'yeah, sure' & she saddles up a couple. It doesn't take her long to see i don't know one end of the thing from the other so she shows me how to put my

    left foot in the stirrup & swing my right leg over & how to use my leg muscles to hold up my body instead of just plopping along on my posterior.

        horses running through high brush.
        high brush fingers clawing our legs.
        Alice riding bareback into the lake
        bent low long hair flying, water
        spraying up a silver arc in the sun.

Next day Alice shows up at Jenny and Ray's riding her horse & leading another & says

    'wanna go for a ride?' as if she doesn't care whether i say yes or no but after awhile i learn that's the way she is, acting like she doesn't care when she does.

        coming upon a small indian encampment in the
        bush. boards and boxes stacked against each
        other. newspapers at openings to keep out rain
        and snow. a line strung onto a tree. a pair of
        small torn jeans.

All the long hot summer Alice shows up nearly every day. Sometimes we ride back to her house so she can help with chores & the little kids. At first i sit & read old Archie comics until she's done but then i start helping her figuring she'll get done quicker. Then one day

    it comes to me i'm having fun especially carrying around those fat babies who are so warm and cuddly & look at me with big solemn eyes & smile slow beautiful smiles. But what

    really amazes me, the mother never yells at anybody, not Alice or the little kids or even the dogs when they track in mud.

> my sisters and i arguing about whose turn it is to do the dishes. mom yelling at us to stop the nonsense or else but we don't stop. nor do we ever find out what the 'or else' is.

One morning Jenny says 'd'y'wanta go with Ray to take supplies to the ranger so i say

    'yeah, sure, can Alice come too' so we pile into the cab of the half ton & start up the mountain where we come upon some men clearing trees, others working with cats & graders.

    Ray stops the truck & gets out & rolls a cigarette & stands jawing with Alice's dad who's foreman of the construction crew building a road. The men talk & smoke & spit & seem to be discussing something of great importance. Ray rolls another cigarette & i figure it's going to be a long wait in that hot cab so i switch on the radio & who comes on but Wilf Carter

singing *I'm in the jailhouse now* which turns out to be Alice's dad's favourite too so we sing along with Wilf our two voices blending together pretty good: *they told me once or twice,*

quit playing cards and shooting dice...

After a long bumpy ride we get to the tower & climb a million steps up to the top where there's

a cozy little one-room house with cupboards & a table & bed. Ray unloads supplies while the ranger who's so old his face is like a map of rivers makes tea on his hot plate. He lets Alice

& me look through his binoculars out over the trees, out over the lakes & rivers, hundreds of miles in all directions, so many trees, trees i would get lost in & never find my way

out of. Ray comes & stands beside me & starts pointing out the best places for hunting & fishing. He names all the rivers & streams & lakes & shows me how they run into each other &

make a pattern. He names the trees & tells me how the boreal forest is like a green necklace around the northern hemisphere & that's when it comes to me, when i'm twelve years

old drinking warm pop in a funny little tree house high up above everything, how this is Ray's country, Ray & Alice & the man in the tower

& Alice's mom & dad & fat little roly-poly

    brothers & sisters, how they know it & feel it in their bones & aren't afraid of getting lost in it & never finding their way out, how they've never lived any place else for ten thousand

    years, how i'm a visitor just passing through.

        postscript: lying on the sand with Alice telling me how when she grows up she's going to go to school & learn how to help her people. but i left at the end of summer & never saw her again so i don't know if she ever did.

a sort of life

travelling eighty miles of dirt road after rain
to find your brother who is lost
on a homestead up around Padstow*

it is 1939 and you are riding a bicycle
manoeuvring through sculpted ruts
carved from gumbo
    that wicked wily clay of the north

you know something about mud
    having survived the trenches
    we were maybe a hundred yards from the germans
      close enough to hear them holler to each other
        hear their bullets whistle over our heads
  we were changing position
      going from one line of trenches to another
        marching single file
          along a ridge
            when we got fired on
i heard a thud behind me and turned around
  there was my buddy shot dead

just like that

one second alive the next dead

i've always wondered

why him and not me

after that you went to all the funerals

    brought flowers on sundays to the graves

after that you knew there was a conversation

    between the living and the dead

after that you couldn't stand the cold

twenty years later you are squatting in snow

    in a place you never thought you'd be

your arm is around my sister

    she in snowsuit with her little toy broom

you are wearing your tweed flat top cap

    the one you wore all through my childhood

behind you in the background Babe

    stretching her neck stealing hay from the barn loft

before mud or snow

    you are reading by candlelight in another country

        a room with papered walls

        table with fancy cloth

            lace curtains at the window

                                      sideboard with crystal decanter
you are sitting on a wicker chair
wearing jacket, tie, breeches, long socks, polished boots
        a schoolboy is our curly headed red-haired jack

                To Master J. McClintock, Belfast.
                Ballyconnell 30/9/06 Dear Jack
                I am going home at end of week. Do
                you know this place (Ramelton Co.
                Donegal.) I was in the fair yesterday.
                Lex

you are some place in France
posing before a fake rose trellis
you are wearing fur tunic with belt
        soldier's hat and boots
                puttees precisely wound from ankle to knee
you are looking at the camera
        maybe you are smiling

                              England, 1915
                To Mr. Hugh McClintock
                Edmonton, Alberta Canada
                Dear Father.

This is the famous Brighton Pavilion "Hindoo
Designs" erected by Albert consort to the Late
Queen Victoria. Brighton is only 8 miles from
Shoreham and I go there constantly. We are
having some of the usual Old Country weather.
It has not stopped raining during the last few
days. I would sooner have "King Zero" than
this. It gets your Goat and makes you feel
miserable. I don't think you could live in this
again on a Bet. However we don't do any
Parades when its raining.
Jack

you are riding through dark streets
                after the evening shift
a thin line of light still on the northern horizon
you are wearing your cap your plaid jacket
           your tan-coloured
                  cork-soled shoes
                          go round and round
      like clock hands circling time
you pass unlighted store windows
        silent alleys
               deserted streets

                       the corner of 111th and 95th
an open window a radio playing
        tommy dorsey swing
a lighted window a man brushing his teeth
a back door a woman putting out the cat

you are sitting in a wheelchair on a balcony
        holding my sister's hand
                the one in snowsuit sixty years away
you are wearing hospice gown and robe
i bend to kiss your cheek and see
        scalp through your once-thick hair
                beard stubble on your chin
                        as if they are afraid to cut too close
                              fragile as tissue paper skin

we sit through the descending afternoon
        as always you keep up your end of things
                making small talk between silences
until you say *I'm so cold*

                I have to go in now

*Aug. 4. Jack came out in ev. We worked in potato patch. 5. L. & J. started wood shed. Letter from Sedor ordered cows out of his pasture. 6. L. Went to Mayerthorpe to see about Babe's shoulder. Jack went up to settle about plows. 7. Bob & Jack worked on pasture fence. 8. Jack & Bob worked some more on pasture fence. 9. We went to hear Kuhls speech & lantern slide show. 10. We went to river in evening. I took a picture. 11. Jack & I & kids went to show. I got sack of flour. The show was very good. Theme - The Girl of the Golden West. 12. We went to river & got more wash water. 13. Jack went back to Ed.

(Diary of a farm wife, 1939)

For Muff Mattson

working on the Gap
        between Exshaw and Canmore
pick and shovel job that was
        building up the Banff highway
            sloping up the banks
 we had some terrible floods up there in those years
        twenty-nine, thirty, thirty-one
Merrion Steam Shovel got a government contract
        to dig a ditch down from the quarry
joe wright from Cochrane was foreman
        he'd been a butcher
            timekeeper was alex mcinnon
we stayed in tents with wood floor sides 4 ft canvas
        coal heater in the middle
$5 a month and had to buy our own tobacco
they fed us but we went on strike in 1933 because of the damn cook
        coughing and dropping cigarette ashes in the soup

Canada Cement owned the town
        they shut down tight in '32
so then you had 200 guys on relief
for a while most people who were laid off got jobs digging

but then they got work on the government highway
I was 13 when we moved to Exshaw
my dad got a job as blacksmith at Canada Cement
when they shut down he was out of a job
              with eight kids to feed
me being the oldest
        I got a job as fireman at the Exshaw hotel

I started playing in the band at the hotel
        and Sarah Dobson's hash house
                drums, taught myself
                        everyone taught themselves in those days
                      you just picked up an instrument and started playing

I worked at a dozen more places over the years
but I always kept up with music and bands
you hadda do something after work Saturday night
we still meet for jam sessions
bunch of us old guys
we've picked up some girls along the way
well we've had women's lib so I guess they're as good as the men
                      our better halves as they say
once a month we pick a band from jammers
        have a regular dance

                usually get out 60 or 70 oldtimers like ourselves
oh no you can't quit music
      no more'n you can quit life

Camus has no heros

like a surgeon touches scars
like a baker touches dough
like a seamstress touches fabric
like a potter touches clay
he touches wood
blindfolded he can tell
pine, maple, oak, spruce
hard from soft
trusting his measurement
without hesitation
        making the cut
you might say with each act defining himself

his hands
the hands of a carpenter
        thick wrists hanging from short jacket sleeves
        each knob of bone clear and distinct

a shy man
a solitary man
on the sofa close beside his wife
a thin man

        although not so thin as she
                she with terminal bone cancer
they married late
        it looked like no one was going to ask her and then he did
        and then the first child came early

our intellectual friends
                debate existence and essence and which is prior
a throwback to our university days
        how we loved to talk about this stuff
        in the lower level reading room of the old library
        where you could cut the smoke with a knife
        and the waste baskets overflowed with paper coffee cups

those who argue for destiny
        are shouted down by those who say
                the myth of destiny leads people astray
leads some to think they're napoleons
        and that can get you into a whole lot of trouble
we're neither heros nor victims of fate says the one who teaches philosophy
        our lives are not written in our bones
                we have a choice

you can't act against yourself someone else says

you must be able to act against yourself otherwise you don't have a choice
                                                  another says
we can't evaluate another person's choice since we must choose from our own reality and each one of us has a different reality, the one who went into street ministry says

we are in an absurd meaningless universe where the only sensible choice is suicide gesticulates the wild haired academic who as a wild haired student memorized each page of the text then tested himself by tearing it out and up

on the sofa
he draws her bones closer into his bones
touches her shoulder as if
        touching wood

the glorious twelfth*

oh the poor dears
they blew up the route this year
today at the Stampede parade
    i thought of the glorious twelfth
        and i said to the guy standing next to me
        we don't have to worry about that here
        i'm irish but I don't like that blowing up stuff

        August 25. Bert arrived 11 o'clock (pm).
        26. Bob & Bert took cows and calves to
        Alvin's. 27. We started washing & packing.
        We put in busy day. 29. Still washing &
        packing. Bert got mail. 30. Still washing &
        packing.
        (Diary of a farm wife, 1939)

    he shows up
  on my doorstep
uncle Bert's little morris chugs into the driveway
    on board
        Malcolm the mutt who's even older than he
            sometimes the girlfriend Orn
      a retired nurse with clamped jaw   smile a shiver

                      of soft muscle riffling loose skin
              without warning
on his way to the coast
    i used to know a lot of people in Victoria
        but it doesn't have the class it used to have

or back from fishing
    these young kids need comfort
                soft mattresses
    i just park my car out in the bush and go to sleep
        i'm better off
            outside of towns
    i might get me a house on the north mountain
                i don't need the electric
    but it's nice to have the plumbing

once he gave me a ring from the bus station to come and get him
he'd killed a moose on the Banff highway
totalled his car
once on a lonely stretch near Moosimin
        the wind blew him clean off the road   airborne
            in the middle of Saskatchewan
                a virtual Pecos Bill
some young people came along and found him

    flipped into the ditch in his volkswagen van that time
        small wheels no ballast
        a white-haired leprechaun
            hanging upside down still clutching the wheel

(when I was a child and lived in the solemn house
    he would come from faraway exotic places
like a character in a noel coward play
smoked and took a drink and had girlfriends and
    was the most absolutely thrilling
        sophisticated creature i had ever met so far)
    after a night's rest he's good as new and on his way
      i'm glad we had this little talk
      now i don't feel so lonely
      i don't mind so much
      going back to an empty house
      for awhile after Alex died it was terrible
      but i'm getting used to being alone
    he adjusts his teeth and for a moment his face unhinges

        To Bertie from Givrauval
        (Meuse) 1916. This is just
        outside the village I am
        living in. Lex

at the door he shows the kids his camping equipment

    what d'y'think eh do i have enough stuff

    you see i have this twine, i braided some

    and this plastic bottle full of sand for an anchor

        and i have my old pots

lets christopher hold in the cupped palm of his small hand

                  a dead bee

2.

before bed the ritual tea and biscuit
reminds him of the way things used to be
when they were all together in the house they built

                he and his brothers

quiet talk around the kitchen table in the yellow light

    there's just joe in granny's old room

    i had another fellow in this winter

        but he was always coming in smelling of beer

                and his feet stank up the place

    he changed his socks and carried his laundry out to the back porch

        but it didn't help

    i put his mattress out on the grass to air

        but it started to rain and oh it's a lot of bother

        so now there's just joe

            but he's so fussy

and always complaining about his aches and pains
you know me, I like to have fruit around the house, you know that
i put it in front of him and he turns up his nose
says he can't eat that
all he does is drink tea slops all day
just like grandfather

i got the roof fixed last spring
painted up the place and it's paid for so why do i want
to fool around with boarders
it's not worth it
lock up and take off when i want to
just turn the key in the lock and go
i think i'll get rid of joe

i make up his bed in the spare room
 make sure he has a glass of water for the night
  warm blankets in case he gets cold
   and especially bring out the fresh crisp white sheets
    the way he used to do for me on weekend visits
     when I was twelve years old and needed him

*February 1939. 4. Bert came to see me. 5. Mother came to see me and mailed my letter. I got up in ev. 6. I was up all day. Dr. Geggie said he thought I could go to mothers next day. Mrs. Grey went home. 7. The nurses brought me my clothes but Dr. Greggie wouldn't let me go because the baby wasn't gaining fast enough. 8. Dr. Richard drove me to mothers. It was very cold but I didn't feel the cold. 9. It was 49 below in morning. I got a letter from Louis advising me against coming home before the weather warmed up. 10. The weather was still very cold. 11. The weather got colder than the day before. 12. Katie Mueller came to see me. We spent a very pleasant afternoon. 13. We read of Mr. Bethels sudden death. It was in the journal. 14. I baked two cakes for Bert. The weather warmed towards evening. 15. The weather was very much warmer. 16. Snowing lightly though not cold. Bert went to Mr. Bethels funeral. 17. The weather was very warm. I came out on the train & Betchers brought me to Hansens. 18. Louis came to Hansens this afternoon. He said Queenie had a heifer calf on Thursday. 19. We came home.

     (Diary of a farm wife, 1939)

5

The bird with feathers of blue
Is waiting for you
Back in your own backyard
    (Billy Rose, Al Jolson, Dave
Dreyer, *Back in Your Own Backyard*)

checking the trap line

cheeky saucy chatty squirrel
leaps through sparrow scold
last summer's grass
to pad spring's nest
morning shopping spree
       acorns beneath brendan's spruce
       hyacinth bulbs left out to ripen
making your rounds
buckthorn   fence   ivan's ash
six-foot leaps
claw/hook
elm's rough bark
flattened pelt never a miss

raucous rowdy unruly chatterbox
throaty caw
impudent unsweet song
stomp and scamper on my head
porch roof to balcony rail
       to acrobatics on telephone cables
entertaining yourself? or us?
checking out the neighbourhood or
just passing through?

sunrise on snow

through the apple tree
leaves that didn't fall this year
the bench that in summer blossomed red and blue

                                      gardenia, anemone

snow-pillowed chair where you sat
reading, the birthday tulips still on the table
red tulips on a red and blue checked cloth

                  on which everything depends

the purple candle, your elbows, your book
you are reading and eating
forking the odd mouthful
your head shining under the light
the same yellow light of my grandmother's kitchen
those war years when they gathered around the blue painted table
on blue painted chairs to listen to the voice of the BBC
its blow by blow account of battles
uprisings, insurgencies, ships lost, planes down, numbers of casualties

                        my uncle's ship lost in the North Atlantic

they were great readers that lot
at the kitchen table with hotted pot and biscuits
by floor lamp in the living room

books open on laps
when the news came on heads lifting
like animals sensing danger

all summer long you sat in the sun with two faces
                              you immortalized
    one with bushy eyebrows, sloppy lips, fierce teeth
            one with drooping eyelids, lolo lips set to receive a kiss
both now with winter heads
        time went so fast
        under the lantern's yellow light

and even though their efforts have been mediocre
their successes not great
they're still here
    they got up this morning
    completed chores
        shovelled the snow
        spoke with neighbours
they have eaten and digested
                        again
they have once more raised their glasses high
            loved again
it may not be much but it is something

early snow

poor little ghosts
hanging from branches
you didn't count on this cold
the leaves leaving

this country is hard on ghosts
                and other creatures
who depend on myth and magic

the importance of ghosts:
        we need them to tell us
                time doesn't exist
it's all the same
this year or fifty years in any direction
yesterday today and tomorrow

        ghosts running across lawns
                could be the ghosts of any year
        tripping over white sheets
                      holes cut for eyes
                            loot bags swinging
        it happened again this October just like last

    ghosts darting through hedges
        designating territory
            the place where we found ourselves
              here in the colonies

            i look behind me
and there you are standing on the sidewalk smoking
a ghost watching ghosts and I say
    what are you doing in my poem
and you say, *i am your poem* *

---

*Jan. 19. I went to Mayerthorpe with Neil & Nels & found that Dr. Craig was closing hospital & going away. I got a slip from Wilkie which he said would get me into R.A. Hosp. 20. I took train to Ed(monton). Pains started an hour after I got there & continued until twelve o'clock. 21. Dr. Geggie said they would try to hurry things up. I was sick all afternoon & lay in case room all night but it didn't do any good. Dr. Richard came to see me in evening. 22. They moved me into big ward early in morn. I was very sick. 23. I was still very sick & they gave me an interveinous (sic). 24. I still couldn't eat anything. Had two interveinouses (sic). 25. Better today &

eating a little. Had an interveinous (sic). 26. Got a letter from Louis which settled my nerves. I was up all day. 27. After plenty of walking around & more treatments my baby girl was born at half past-seven in ev. 28. Feeling fairly well after a good sleep. 29. Feeling as well as can be expected, Bert & mother came to see me. Weather very cold.

       (Diary of a farm wife, 1939)

thoughts while wandering the wasteland of the Bay bedding

each morning i get up thinking this will be the day
                                   i'll put off death
each afternoon
about five o'clock i declare my defeat

drifting aimlessly in the city of the dead
thinking maybe tomorrow i'll get on with the work
of remembering how to be happy
right now wallowing in death
seems to be my job

each morning the promise
         a clean perfect slate ahead and maybe the sun's shining
then before i even stand up, swing feet to floor, i'm thinking things like
what did adam and eve take with them when they left paradise
and were they tormented with might have beens

i can't get you out of my mind
or the fellow at the intersection
on his way to work on an ordinary morning in spring
waiting at the yield sign for an opening in traffic
when suddenly coming straight at him

across the median, a cube van

lands right on top of him

killing him dead on the spot

at home a young wife

an 18 month old child

my fed-up friends say
        i don't want to get out of this dark hole i've fallen into
            and when i think of it
                they're right
i don't want to leave you in that place all alone
            you were always afraid of the dark

6

> ...seeking a place to stand
> or a place to hide...
> (Don Henley, Glenn Frey,
> *The Last Resort*)

crouching in the cabbage patch like a whiskers trembling rabbit

                                                       (for the poets)

                  here i come
says the poet tiptoeing along the rows
                          there's no escape

hearing my footsteps your ears stiffen
the merest vibrations of earth might send you scurrying
and what if you have to sneeze, what if you can't hold it back
although you are a master at this game and where did you learn it
was it at the orphanage, behind the garden shed
                          or in the cool green between houses
                                the last days of equilibrium
                                        before the war and refugee camps
where you played the hiding game to keep the little kids quiet
so the guard with the big stick wouldn't find you

is that you peeking around the corner of the garage
your eyes brown pools and what's at the bottom
                            not fear or even evasion
challenge and defiance are hiding places too but it's neither
your eyes brim with glee because you've fooled us all
                                    all of us who could not find you
                            in your conundrums

                your mazes and games of language
           your desire to please not strong enough
                to destroy your desire to hold yourself intact
once you stayed hidden for hours in the squash
beneath huge leaves floating like a green lake above you
                      a sort of autistic retreat
               lovely and cool in the shade near the earth
alerted when the voices came close
      she must be here some place
      it's time for supper
      it's time for bed

      oh come on, let's go, let's play another game
said Lil of the bored voice
the same voice that said *do you have to go into all that detail*
      it's the only way i can remember you said
      one thing leading to another
was it scorn like hers turned you into reluctant matter

the voices leave and the footsteps leave and you are alone
      with your hiding
           silence turned inside out on itself
but maybe you want to be found
      maybe you are waiting for someone to say *it's all right*

>*you can come out now*

maybe you want someone to take you by the hand

bring you into the lighted kitchen in the early autumn evening

        to join the others around the table

                hot chocolate moustache

                        marshmallow chin

Mr. Manning's Back to the Bible Hour

we get dressed up in our Sunday best which isn't all that great but what the
       hell we think it is.
          and led by Chrissie in her blue blazer and pleated skirt and
          clutching her purse and her
bible in her fat freckled hand march off to the bus stop. Chrissie never
       makes it to service because
she meets this guy which is the real reason she likes to supervise the trip
       down to the Strand theatre for back to bible hour. so then she and
       this guy (who i don't trust no further than
i can throw but i'm nine years old and Chrissie is sixteen so compared to
       her what do i know about guys) take off somewhere but not
       before Chrissie gives us strict orders about meeting
outside the theatre again in an hour and we'd better be there or else. but it
       doesn't matter if we're late because she's always later and that's
       okay since we're the last ones out on account of
       getting saved which we do every Sunday.

i follow the older kids who get up all in a row and in pious procession to
the tune of *softly and*
       tenderly Jesus is calling descend the sloping aisle to the front where
we kneel with some other people of course and a preacher of which there
are several some all the way from Oklahoma

    which i'm not sure where it is talks to us about giving up our sinful ways and taking the Lord Jesus Christ into our hearts. i have to say i really like getting saved. for one thing i really dig

    the music, *'come home, come ho...o...ome, you who are weary come home,'* because even though i'm only nine i'm pretty weary of my life being in the orphanage and all. also it's

    an adventure to walk down the aisle of the big theatre in front of all those people and have a grown-up take you seriously and ask questions like are you ready to meet your saviour.

still we don't have as much fun as the catholics at least what my friend at school says they

    have. when they go down to the front of the church they get something to eat like a biscuit or wafer. but it's better than staying home with the little kids who sit in the sandbox sifting sand

    hour after hour. or if it isn't raining sitting on the swing watching the trains go by trying to think where all those people in the windows are going but not able to because you can't imagine a

    place you've never heard of just like you can't imagine freedom if you've never had it.

midnight shift. weather station north of 50

or:

loneliness of the long distance writer

or:

where the ashtrays are always full and the coffee cups empty

or:

her first real job after waiting tables and working at Woolworth's

or:

marking time until her life starts

the pilots come for their briefing.

storm coats and snow boots flapped open

defy sleet whipped by the wind into horizontal sheets.

stars invisible. no direction home.

their quiet voices.

if we wait for it to stop we'll hafta wait til spring.

the challenge keeps them alive.

love is flying into the unknown

                                        hiding in a duck blind

                              some say he's black but i say he's bonnie

                                hot tomato soup in the thermos

                                    bologna sandwiches

revolving tower lights slice snow like a scythe
    swathes hay in a kinder season.
slice bodies spilling from the terminal.
a thin straggling dribble down on the tarmac.
huddled shapes hunched into coat collars
    hang on to hats hand luggage swaddled babies.
propeller's whir and scream. the great grey whale swims
    along the runway. disappears
        into white. you can only imagine wheels lifting
folding. the huge thrust up.

        an airplane drones in the overhead darkness
        how much more i cannot see
        you coming up the walk in your hunting gear

behind her a lone teletype shuffles into action.
some poor bastard who drew isolation
snowbound in a howling blizzard
polar bears nosing around his cabin
clicks his message to the planet.
there's something hiding here at the end of the line
something that won't budge
something i can't see. 500 miles into tundra
he receives her communication at the moment of each key stroke.

> *i know where I'm goin'*
> *and i know who's goin' with me*
> time to get up sweetie
> hollow flap of gas, hiss & blue flame
>   toast and eggs and coffee...

tonight Ruby has Fort Smith.
her knitting needles click in rhythm to machine clack.
silver screen romance propped on her teletype ledge.
without losing a stitch in her scarf or a word of her romance
    she rips off an incoming tape
        plays it on to Winnipeg and points east
keeps up a steady stream of gossip about the stars.

> *i know who i love*
>   *but the dear knows who i'll...*
> talk in quiet voices. pad the floor in heavy socks.
> pile on layers: underwear, slacks, sweater, boots.
> the jaunty little cap he bought her.

Walter the war casualty doped up for pain
has Norman Wells. reaches with his cane
flicks a switch and starts the weather moving north
while the gangrene creeps higher.

while the cutoff creeps higher.

raises his bad leg to a chair. raises a flask from his hip pocket.

what is waiting in the blizzard. in the frozen landscape.

travelling as suspension of reality

                before dawn the streetlights all have halos.

                    the dial of the car radio glows red. the

              supermarket is a giant passenger ship

            floating toward them out of the mist.

            oh the tires they hum

            the songs they sing for each other.

Harley's a man who plays by the rules.

when a dozen machines go crazy spouting constant streams of weather

and systems go down and you have a dozen tapes clipped onto the front of

    your machine

waiting for a break in traffic and some guy in, say, Saskatoon

feeds in one tape on the tail of another hogging the line

not giving you a chance to clear yours

some operators cheat and start their tapes before

the scheduled time but never Harley. eye on clock.

finger on switch. countdown of seconds. we're on.
twirl and dance. lightly on his feet.

love as suspension of reality

        standing in the swamp in their rubber boots
           drizzle down their faces
           crouching in the ditches
              they are happy

        cold and wet they build
           a fire in their sheltered grove
           drink soup hot from the thermos.
              he puts down his coat for her to sit on.

brown bagging it with Keith in the lunch room.
their story (according to Ruby):
Keith and June newly arrived in the city
boarded at the same house and he got her pregnant so
they had to get married and now
they have three kids and
always some month left at the end of the money and
he's trying to get transferred to a remote station further north
where he can draw isolation pay. but what if the electricity stops
she says or your supplies don't make it in.

what if the planet goes dead

and you're the only survivor and you don't even know it.

what bothers me... his words and his salt sift down in slow motion

...what if I get to like it.

love is dangerous

                                    he teaches her how to walk with a gun.

                                       how not to walk with a loaded gun.

travelling as suspension of reality

this guy steals a plane to go to Ireland

but needs to make a stop in the States to get some money

to pay for his girlfriend's divorce. in Great Falls

he picks up 50 thousand and lets the passengers go

except for one stewardess he holds hostage.

        airborne again they'll fly over

heading for the arctic circle. the news from the tower.

he has been subdued by the crew. then a minute

by minute report of the plane's approach.

visibility is the shits can't see fuck all.

we're lost up here, you're gonna hafta help us in man.

arrival as reality

air traffic control gets him down.
red lights flash close closer. sirens, police, ambulance.
RCMP mount the ramp. wait for the doors to open.
two paramedics enter the plane come out carrying a stretcher.
figure wrapped and belted in. white band around his head.
i hope she was worth it says Harley watching through the window.

                        they come to a place of dead things.
                        bleached skeletons. carcasses of trees.
                        they wade in stagnant slough water
                              up to their knees.

on her coffee break she visits him in his tower.
their smoke entwines. spirals upward in a lazy dance.
you knew all the good spots she says. *you knew each tree stump*
fence post, ditch. here's the place we bagged two pheasant last year.
here's the side road where we parked to wait for the light
and drink one thermos and smoke one cigarette.
you're my hunting buddy he says. *best one i ever had.*
i'd better get back she says. *Ruby will be wanting her break.*

                        a bird lands with a thud on rotting leaves.
                        the dog brings them the dead bird.

                lays it at their feet. shakes himself.
                sprays them with putrid water.

arrival as reality

a thin line of light on the horizon.
the unwrinkled day shift drifts in. women in fresh makeup
men clean shaven. night shift with five o'clock shadow
lipstick smeared by lunches and chocolate bars
breath smelling of endless cups of coffee and cigarettes
clothes stale and slept in. drifts out.

                fairest of them all
                    is my handsome winsome...

in the washroom mirror she looks into her eyes.
leaves without picking up her pay. hitches a ride south.
the band around her head loosens with each mile.

7

PostScript

found poems

Dancing

Every Saturday afternoon from 2:00 to 4:00
               at the   Sponsored by

                                           Heintzman & Co. Ltd.

       Rendezvous
    7th Av. at 4th St. W.
      Saturday afternoon swing club
Buy yourself a War Savings Stamp as Your Admission

Leaving

18. Jim came down in evening to start cutting. Bob hauled two loads of water from Ward. Bob & Alvin came in ev. 19. Jim cut all day. 20. Jim cut. B. hauled 2 more loads water. I took some pictures. 21. Charlie Kezar and Karl came down to stook. Jim broke a part on binder & had to go to Mayerthorpe. Bob hauled one load water. 22. B. emptied the ward well after half filling tank. Went to B. W's. for load in aft. Got letters from mother, Louis & Jack ex. accident. Took picture of binder in oats. Jim finished cutting. Charlie & Karl left that night. 23. Jim pulled outfit home. B. & I finished stooking in ev. 24. I had headache all day. Georgina & Patsey were here in aft. We went to Scotts in ev. & watered horses at ward well. 25. B hauled load of water for washing. Mar was here all aft. I got bee sting after supper. Bert arrived 11 o'clock. 26. Mar. came up & helped me wash. Bert went for walk. Bob hauled more water. 27. We went visiting, had dinner at Gingers, called at all places along road. We went to McClures. Hansens were at Brida's when we got back. 28. We started washing & packing. We put in busy day. 29. Still washing & packing. Bob went to Rochfort. Bert got mail. 30. Still washing & packing. Bob & Bert took cows & calves to Alvins. Mary E. & Lily came back with them. 31. We took treble sewing machine, washing machine & pig to Scotts. Hansens came & then Jim, Brida & Charlie Kezar. We finished our goodbyes almost tearfully.

Sep. 1. We killed chickens & did the last finishing work of packing & preparing for a long trip.

> (Diary of a farm wife, 1939)

END

126